Today's Eco-Friendly Family

Creative Ways to Live Simply &
Sustainably for Our Children and theirs!

Zuki Abbott

For my Son Zack and my Grandson Taillis.

For your children and theirs and for the planet
Mother Earth we call home!

Contents

Disclaimer:

The purpose of this book is to share suggestions and ideas for a simple way of living and saving the planet for our children.

In no way is the publisher or any associations of this book, trying to endorse or prescribe any alternative to one's own health care process or to aid in giving any medical advice.

It is you the reader, an adult who can choose what is right for you and no one else. We encourage research and in depth decision making when it comes to your own well-being, health and life issues.

We take no credit or blame for anything we share in this book.

Acknowledgments:

This book is one of my hopes to help manifest one of the most important aspects of living, in a world today of consumerism. Creating a new paradigm for our children's future and for this to be created by all who love the children and our Mother Earth!

I want to thank all who supported me alongside on this journey of self-discovery. Most importantly my son Zack and his son Taillis for being my best guys in this life. And of course my dear husband Nicholas for always supporting my sane and not so sane ideas and creativity on a whim.

I love you all!

Introduction:

More and more today we are hearing about living simply. Tiny homes, living 'off grid' and the slew of media attention on 'family DIY birth.' A lot is changing, and to help flow with the change we need to learn how to help assist in it, in a way that benefits all humanity. The in 'the' moment gratification, throw-away society is just not working for the future of our planet. And for our children's future children's health and wellbeing.

The way we have been living for the past few decades is just not sustainable for the majority of us who work all the time and who have young children. We are slaving away sacrificing our time with our families, and our true callings. In order to buy basic things we used to think were necessary to live, are becoming more and more evident there needs to be change.

There are solutions to lessen the effects of stress and live simply so our children can have us while they are young and to grow and learn better ways of living themselves. Hopefully in a world without struggle to survive. We need to THRIVE!

"We do not inherit the Earth from our Ancestors; we borrow it from our Children."

~Ancient Indian Proverb

Chapter One

Simple Ways to Become Eco-Friendly Families

Basic Eco-Friendly Family Principles:

Simplicity: Living simply, not necessarily in a tent or tiny house, but it could be for you. It really is a feeling of freedom when you live that way for a while or for a lifetime. Being close to nature, in balance or learning to be. It is very rewarding on so many levels. Not having to work all the time just to buy the newest TV or technology, make it basic. Use what you need, reuse things and recycle. Think twice about that new pair of shoes or jacket. Buy from thrift shops or second hand stores and maybe even learning to make your own clothes can be fun and good to teach the children. It does not have to be like sacrificing your standards or your desires. This can be a small way to lessen the consumption on the planet, and save money. Which feels good inside and out!

That is how I see it and it works for me and many I know. And we can still dress nice and have nice things, they are just things that have been used before us, and are a lot less expensive. What do we truly need? When I think about what my family needs when we go shopping I write a list maybe two. I may lose one or forget it at home, but it is written.

What we need and want or desire, are all very different, but we can get what we need and sometimes what we desire by having a priority list. Sometimes I write one than go over it with my son and husband and whoever else is involved. I ask, "Do you really need that?" If the answer is yes then so be it, if not and we waiver then we cross it off the list. We all need a few simple things; Food, Shelter, Warmth, Water to bathe and cook with, and of course LOVE. The basics. All of us on our wonderful planet can have these basic human needs met.

If we can do our best to think simply and get what we need, we can sometimes get what we want too. Also after doing this for some time there is a time and place for desires, because we saved money on not buying things we don't really need. Also taking into consideration other's needs. If we all chose to adopt a person in need, feed and share our abundance with and possibly even help them find proper care and shelter so they can also live in balance, we would all benefit! No one should be homeless or starving. No one should have to suffer in this world of plenty! We all just need to learn to minimize what we personally consume and share the wealth of clothing, food, water, and shelter. We can do it!

Creativity: Creating abundance through saving and reusing items that are thrown away. Clothes for example; you can use old clothes to make new clothes, diapers, cleaning rags, curtains, purses, dolls clothes, hats, mittens, blankets, so much creative re-using. Saving on factory made things, saving money and making the world a more colorful place to live! Some other ideas I have experimented with are using old magazine pictures to wall paper rooms over the years, front doors, walls, floors, tables, chairs. You can basically make collages on anything and it's fun, colorful and creative. What a great way to decorate and recycle beautiful art in old magazines and calendars. It is a great way to spend time with the kids too. They can create their own dream boards, goal boards, chore boards, idea boards, and posters for their rooms.

Use this time to help improve the living space. Try to find one project per week that is not too time consuming to have fun and enjoy one another's company and recycle something. Paint an old dresser or walls in a room. Maybe clean out old storage sheds or attics and basements to find projects to do with the family and have a sale or keep it for yourself.

Reusing and recycling is a fun and creative form of family time. I feel this also teaches kids to be mindful of not throwing things away but taking care of things they have, and use for a lifetime if they do. I am not endorsing hoarding, but taking care of items that can be used, fixed up and re-used, not feeling like we always have to go out and buy new furniture or clothes just because we can. These fun family projects will become, Eco-Friendly Family Heirlooms!

Sensibility: Using Eco-Friendly ways to live. Creating a dynamic in our minds that suits the lifestyle we would like and In-Joy. Being 'sensible' is different for each individual. As long as we can discuss with ourselves if something is truly needed or just wanted or desired and figure out which would benefit you and your family in the long run. Not just in the moment, then we will not be making choices that may not improve our lives. Gratification in the moment can sometimes be needed or desired. It is fine to do this now and then. Have an ice cream cone if that is your desire in this moment. However, how we are raised in this culture of self-serving and momentary gratification, consumerism is downright greedy behavior, has had a poor impact on the planet and on our humanness. Create priority lists of what you would like to see change in your day to day life and share it with your family. Ask for support, ask everyone to also write their priority list and share it. Being sensible is not always the same for everyone. We can think we have a certain priority, then when we write it down and share it, we can ask from those around us who live with us what their opinion is about our lists and get feedback. If we are to make sensible changes we need to begin simply. Is it sensible to want a steak every night for dinner? Maybe not, but if you live on a farm and have cows maybe it is.

Again, priority lists are useful to figure out what your reasons are for feeling that you need something or not. If we can take a moment and not impulse buy, we can eliminate over fifty percent of unnecessary buying! It worked for me anyway. I like to think I am frugal, and at times I am not, I recognize this within myself, depends on the decisions I make when I stop and think about if I really need or want something. Most of the time, I can talk myself out of things and feel good about that choice. The important things such as health care items or food need to be bought. But new furniture, clothes (I try to buy used) and items I do not need such as nick knacks or jewelry, makeup, stuff like that, I do not give into. I much rather wait and save money to go on vacation or go out to dinner or see a show now and then. That is my priority. We usually give ourselves space to think about if we truly need something out of want or if it is seriously needed for school, work or the house for improvements or maintence. It is OK to want things from time to time. But think sensibly.

Co-Operation: 'Co'-Meaning; Together, community, communal, 'Co' OPERATIVE to 'unite,' creating family, sustainability and sensible living or simple living begins with co-operation. Co-operating with ones-self or with one's child or family or community is essential to survival & sustainability in the long term.

When I was young I had to live communally. It was the only way I could afford to be a single mother and go to school and work and take care of my son full-time. If I had not shared space with others who I could trust to help when I needed to go to a class or go to work for a while I would not have done any of it. I lived with other mothers, grandmothers, grandfathers, friends, peers, and other people's children. We needed to co-operate because it was the only way to get everything everyone needed out of life. Some had their own reasons. One would be to save money; so that someday we would be able to afford to buy our own home, or build it. Buy food instead of go on assistance to do so. Have community of others there for company or like me, to have a family environment to raise my son in and have help when I needed it. I did not always enjoy living with others, but I knew I was searching for that 'back to the village' lifestyle and a part of that is to be able to commune with others.

18

So we did. And for twenty-eight years that is what we did to be able to one day build our own home and have enough saved up to start our gardens and get sustainable.

To me, it is about family and sometimes family comes in ones who are not even blood related. We to this day live communally. But we have plans to build a house so we can in our old age have some time to ourselves when we want it.

The thinking of separation and isolation and 'mine,' is not of benefit to all or to the planet or for the future of our children. Let us shift and change this paradigm so we can all share and get what we need, COMMUNITY.

Foundation: Creating foundation of health for long term sustainability and thriving, not only surviving. A well balanced foundation begins with all of the above basic principles of Eco-Friendly living on the planet and preserving what we have for our children's future. This can mean many things. First, this means to create a foundation of mental, emotional & physical health and well-being for ourselves and therefore for our children who come after us. Everything begins in this moment. Eating healthy, drinking healthy, and being mindful to what we buy or put on or into our bodies is what a foundation would entail. We can try our best to lessen our stress by not over consuming anything to the point of unnecessary waste.

Nutrition and environment do affect us on all levels. Even spiritually we need nourishment. The mind and body can work together if we take care of the basic elements of ourselves. Beginning at conception, birth, choices of parenting, lifestyle, we set the stage for the future health of our children. We can make choices that may benefit them by doing research, finding all options in pregnancy, birth and where and with whom to birth. The time in doing this will benefit not only this pregnancy and birth but those that may come after, and the children those children may also have in their future. We set the imprints in place when making very important decisions about how to care for ourselves while growing our babies and how we will birth them and raise them. A lot of this begins well before conception as we are creating our path along the way to that special day when we find out we are 'with child,' and about to bring forth a New World, and new generations to come. When we speak of 'family base', the 'family core', we are literally speaking of foundation. Setting a base of health and well-being for their future. Like an Heirloom, we keep it clean, polish it and take care of it, mend it if needed along the way and pass it down from our hands to our children's, so they too can pass it down to theirs. With care to teach them how to polish it and take care so it won't break or whither. We must do the same for our children now, with their basic foundations of health, so their future will be abundant and with fewer struggles. Teach them to care for themselves by first caring for yourself and the planet we live on.

The Eco-Friendly Family thrives to sustain. Create health through proper nutrition, prevention through education, support and science based beliefs. We are in 'this' *together*. Sharing and supporting self-reliance, responsibility and In-JOY, so our children can have a brighter future without our distrust of self, ill-health, and financial struggles. Living true to our original gifts we are given. To use our mind, use our plant families for medicine, our animal families sparingly for food, treating our environment, our Mother Earth with great reverence, respect and honoring her as we honor and respect ourselves. Not wasting precious time and money on 'things,' but spending our time and resources for investing in the future of our children's future planet and children.

"We will be known forever by the tracks we leave."

~ Native Indian Proverb

Chapter Two

Creating Eco-Consciousness

Beginning to create new conceptions, literal conception as the beginning of human form of our new family, our new paradigm of life, even the world! For us to have a new beginning of a thought or vision, realizing we are the creators. We can create this new life in love, in joy and very well much a utopia of our choosing if we would like. Utopia to me, is the way I believe we can live in peace and inner joy and harmony with all living beings on our planet. If we can conceive this idea of utopia within ourselves first we can than create it within our families. Birthing them in balance, with peace and within the nature of love. To do this may be a challenge for some as we are not fully recognized as creatures of nature yet. The separation of 'us' and 'them' still runs deep.

We are a part of, not apart from, nature and all its wonderful gifts we have been given since the beginning of time. Our purpose if not realized will be in its 'fullness' or 'prime' by the time we begin our own families, having babies, creating marriages, homes, professions. Our fullest potential is formed before we are even born. The world's dynamics continually try to separate us from our original purpose and create slaves of us. Unfortunately, many are programmed at such an early age. We then forget our original purpose or 'mission' on this planet. We are here to remember.

Did our Creator create us to suffer? Live in fear? Separate us from others and our own children? I personally do not believe this to be true. However, many do, not even realizing it, but act upon it none-the-less. Conditioning from society, family, beliefs, religion and school systems are the foundation of this disbelief that we are here for a purpose. Except for us to serve the system at hand.

Beginning once again to form a thought, create a path, start a new world or paradigm for the rest of our lives, the future of our children's lives and thereafter. This is the PURPOSE of why we are here now. At least one of many.

Vitality of life and the planet begins with us. Each individual counts. We can choose to ignore or choose to do something vitally important for the planet and all who inhabit it. Our sustainability depends on our trust in nature, our love for it, and our dedication to it. We are a part of the entire larger ECO-FAMILY, the planet and all who live on it.

Let's begin simply. Do you find yourself searching for something you cannot explain? Is it a bigger idea or thought that you feel you need in order to shift your life to become whole, happier, and have more abundance? This is something very important to you, your family, your health, your future grandchildren, and our planet earth. You are important, and to realize this you must first accept it as truth. Your contributions to the planet and to others are as important as money, new things, and even your religion. It is above all what we are; loving, compassionate and eco-dynamic creatures. We have brains that function only to the capacity we are told it can. It can work much greater than we let it.

We are not fully using our highest potentials we were given at birth. Somehow, we search. Our primal minds remember even if we do not. We keep searching in hopes that something will come forth and show us how and why. Why are we here and how can we do better?

First, I believe we can do better. Better with our own lives and better with others. We can conceive new ideas, and place them into the perfect order of importance for our own sanity, emotional well-being, physical, mental and spiritual. If we can gather faith that we can, we will.

How do we shift a paradigm? May we be able to do this alone or with a partner or a community? All is true. We can do this in any of these ways by fully opening up to it. The idea that we can and will, from the start, helps to create the reality we thrive to shift. The mind is a powerful tool. We have heard this often growing up but the examples we were given may not have been the best resources of positive creation. Let us try to put behind the ideas we were given and create new ones, right now. Unless the ideas were positive imprints of course. There are some wonderful parents out there who were on top of this.

Think about who instilled the ideas of what life is about to you at an early age. Mother and Father usually. Maybe write down who and what was instilled.

Example: Importance-For me it was behavior, grammar, academia, what I looked like, the clothes I would wear or how fat or skinny I was dictated how I was treated. The importance instilled materialism and appearances rather than how I felt or my talents, thoughts and emotional well-being being the most important. There is a greater picture here to realize. The foundation was missing. I had to re-create my foundation as I realized my purpose. Conditioning, imprinting and eco-unfriendly examples were my first thoughts on this. How do I change this brainwashing?

To me personally, it is important to first care for the emotional-self, mental, physical and spiritual. I began shifting my awareness to these aspects of life when I was very young because nothing else was working. I was not happy. I was merely surviving. No one around me thought it to be an issue but I saw that they were also not happy people. Not the kind of happiness that came from inner joy. There was some happiness from an outer perspective though, not from a deep understanding of purpose. Money played a role in that temporary happiness. Materialistic happiness. The days of joy ended when I was a few years old and realized that the world was not only about singing songs in my grandmother's lap or snuggling with her at night watching tv., it was about struggle. People all around me seemed to be struggling to make money, to buy houses or things that were fashionable. There was sadness at the end of each day when my mother would come home exhausted from working a long day having to care for me. I felt like a burden. Her days were spent working long hours all day, every day. I don't even recall seeing her very much that first half of my life. I was in the care of others. First I was cared for by my extended family, then by strangers. I was afraid. I felt alone. It did not seem like a world of love to me after those few years past. It seemed like a struggle to survive. This first remembrance of struggle left a great imprint on my body and mind. Into young adulthood I had already began a pattern of being in 'survival mode.'

This continued until I realized I did not want to survive, I wanted to do my best and practice reaching my highest potential as a human on earth. Helping others and learning so I could pass on this information for generations that come after me.

In my later years as a teen there was much more struggle and survival, than marriage, a child, divorce and it goes on. I did survive. But I wanted to thrive.

In my early twenties I made a plan to search for a great path. To bring up my son well and healthy, and not dependent on manufactured happiness, but true and raw JOY! My attempts at first were in itself a struggle. Only because I believe the imprints of self-worth had been snuffed out by the nature of how I was exposed to what those around me thought to be true.

I had to get back to nature to find myself. I began living remotely, finding nature in each day to connect with her and her wonders, but not much money. Shifting my paradigm of what was truly needed was a long process. I knew from birthing naturally and 'catching' my son, with my own hands, imprinted great self-reliance in me, that my maternal map was mostly intact. I knew how to do this without a book or others telling me how. My child taught me more than any teacher ever had. To LOVE and TRUST.

The first moments after being born should be surrounded by loved ones who are the ones who will be there to raise, love and nourish this child.

Chapter Three

Becoming Eco-Friendly

As time moved forward and crept into my awareness of something greater than I ever knew or could explain; I wondered around searching, gathering, studying anything to do with nature. Plants, homeopathy, yoga, dance, building with natural materials, emergency survival care, energy healing, body work, birth, death, anything that was about self-reliance, sustainability and hope for the future of human kind.

I felt if I were to choose that path I would fully embrace it and all of its greatness and horribleness, challenges, obstacles and rewards. First I began to live simply. I traveled a lot when I was a young single mother. Living in tents sometimes, our van or at a friends along the way in search of a plot of land to build a home for my son and I. Somewhere I could grow food and make things from materials that were used or otherwise would have been destroyed or thrown away at the dump. I gathered books to learn how to do these things and began by fumbling a lot.

I learned how to make my own soaps, toothpastes, tinctures, salves and clothes. Baked bread by hand, ate vegetarian, vegan and raw at times, to save money but also to be healthier.

As I meditated on our path for Eco-Family Friendly lifestyle, I definitely had challenges. I was a single mother with very little support from anyone. I knew only a few who had similar ideals as I, and they were not my age or lived nearby. No one in my immediate circle of friends had children yet. I was very young, did not have a steady job except being a mother, which to me was the most important job. It is.

I was a full-time student of life, with no one way commitment to any of the things I was studying. I just wanted to learn everything I could. My child was most important, first priority and my goal to be as self-sufficient as possible were my two most important things in life, and still are now.

After realizing that the foundation of my life was now my mission, I began to settle down. Moving around was getting old. My son was eight and he was ready to have community and a family of friends to grow up with. After a long journey from the east coast to the Wild West, I settled down in a very small village town in the Rocky Mountains. I was still dabbling in many aspects of career choices and raising my still young son alone. I needed to find a place in the mountains; my utopia. I found a small but growing community of mostly likeminded people. That was the beginning. Mostly those who wanted to live away from mainstream ideas, build their own homes, grow food, and raise kids in a safe space where they could be kids. Mostly without worry.

By then I had a lot of experience under my belt so to speak. I could craft, give massages, make medicines out of plants, make my own soap, toothpaste, cook, help women in birth, sew a wound, and sow a seed to grow my own food. Now was time to build a house of our own and raise my son with values and an understanding of how to live simply.

It helped to be open minded, and minimalistic learning all I could to take care of myself and my child; always knowing that this would all be for the next generations to come. I made a promise to myself that everything I did would be for the future of the people to come after me, not just for the moment.

All I could learn would be to pass on to the ones after me. This was once told to me as a child by my grandmother. She too was aware and had ideas to help create a better future for others. She gave me a few words that stuck with me for my lifetime.

"Do well not only for yourself but the ones that come after you."
~Helen Abbott

Chapter Four

Eco-Friendly Ways to Act Now

Re-using things has always been a favorite of mine. I learned that if I reuse things, I do not waste as much and I can save money. Here are a few eco-friendly ways to reuse, and feel good about not throwing things into the landfill. Too much today is wasted. With technology being less quality and more of a 'throw it away' buy a 'new' upgrade society; we are faced with serious dilemmas of waste and pollution.

Dish Towels: Instead of paper towels, dish towels can be reused for many months and then used to clean with after they are no longer good to dry dishes with. This saves paper. Trees milled endlessly for paper products are a waste of oxygen and cause pollution in the atmosphere. You can even make dish towels out of old clothes. After using cloth to dry my dishes and use to clean with for a few decades now, I can say that it makes me feel better then when I used to use paper towels. When I did, it was a one-time use then into the trash! My mother did that. Many people I knew growing up used at least five or six rolls of paper towels a week! I would see this waste and wonder what we did before they existed. Of course! Use and reuse cloth.

Plastic Bags: When thinking about buying plastic bags, realize that if you are shopping and gather things in those plastics bags hanging above the lettuce in the produce section, you are able to wash and reuse those bags for other things you may need to put away and store. They are fine to use over and over again. Throwing them away only used once would be wasting a great resource. We use ours over and over again. Once used for food for a while, then to cover a bowl of leftover salad, then we use them for a trash bag. This is one thing that would be so easily changed as a habit, it is right there. Everyone uses those bags and they can be reused over and over.

Another use of these plastic bags, which I have found to be creative, is to weave them into stronger larger bags. Then using them to fill up produce at the grocery store instead of taking home more plastic bags. Creating a way to show others as well, how they too can reuse and minimize their waste.

Cartons: Almond milk, orange juice, milk, whatever kind of carton. Cut one side out of it and use it to plant seed starts! I have done this and it works great. Even better than using those shallow black seed starting trays. Cartons are usable for few uses of seed starting. They do get softer as you use them, then they can be put back into the earth for mulching. You can make bird feeders out of them by doing the same thing. Cutting a portion out of one side, half the side, and pulling a string or fishing line through the top part to hang it. Great project to do with the kids. They can also decorate the bird feeder or paint it. They can also be used as pet feeders. Doing the same thing, they make a great travel size container for watering and feeding your pets on the road. Cartons which are many can also be used for making a money bank. Just cut out the plastic spout and you have a hole large enough to slip money into! Of course wash it out and let fully dry before doing this.

Plastic containers: There are various plastic containers we end up buying food in. We can reuse most of them by washing and using for left overs. Instead of buying new plastic containers, just reuse the ones you buy with food in them. All of these things can improve the quality of life later. First we are not throwing them into the trash which ends up in the landfill and pollutes our environment.

I reuse plastic a lot. I would rather not need plastic at all, but it is here and we are faced with a choice, reuse it or throw it away. Food storage is indefinite use. Others are re-using plastic to start seeds in. You can line into the bottoms of your garden beds for a weed barrier. Putting lots of mulch over it and then your soil. Creating many types of art projects and making signs for around the house with them to remind others of the many uses of plastic.

Old Clothes: I reuse old clothes in a few ways. First the cotton white T-shirts are great to cut down into 'Moon Pads' (Menstrual cloth). It sounds strange, but I can use these over and over each month and then wash them and use as cleaning rags or stuff into projects like making pillows and no one would even see them in their last use! Old clothes can also be made into baby wipes. We can use old clothes again and again. By making new clothes with them, doing creative patchwork projects or blankets, kid's quilts, baby clothes, doll clothes or curtains. So much use out of old clothes.

Sure, if they are in great condition donating them to less fortunate people is a good way of reusing and passing them on. However, a lot of old clothes, socks, underwear even can be reused within their families in all these ways. Socks for instance, we have used to make puppets out of. They can also be dyed and used with other creative projects.

Paper: Look around and see what paper products you acquire and list them. Find out what happens to them in your home. How are they reused? In our home we save any kind of paper product throughout the year to burn in our fire place over the winter as it is our source of warmth. We save it in a large bin. All the junk mail and newspapers that are left at the post office and any kind of paper waste we may accumulate. Other things I use paper for are to make lists on, use in art projects with my grandson and of course paper Mache projects.

We also have a burn bowl in the front of our home so we can enjoy a fire now and then and use our scrap paper to start it. I save certain mail that has personal information on it to burn. I use paper for mulch in my worm bin. Worms love paper in the soil. There are so many uses for paper from creating art projects to lining a cat litter box.

Aluminum Cans: I do not buy or drink out of Aluminum as it is a heavy metal, I do not feel is good for my blood stream. However, a lot of people do use them and then throw them out or hopefully recycle them. I have been collecting aluminum cans for outside projects we have been learning about over the years. One fact I had no idea about until recently, is that you can use them to build walls. I am now fascinated by this idea and we are now using cans to build walls all over the property. Retaining walls, garden walls, and our chicken yard and coop.

After they are built, they are covered over with cob, cement, stucco your choice, and you would have no idea they were made out of cans. Those pretty South Western courtyard walls, a lot of them are adobe, cinder block or can infill. I think the cans are great because you are taking them and using them rather than putting them into a landfill; a place that uses more energy recycling them. Or they get sent over the ocean to other countries to deal with. Evidently you can use cans for many things pertaining to storing energy from the sun. There are plans online you can find that show you how to build your own homemade solar cells with cans. This is something I want to learn more about. Also you can literally build a house with cans. And when covered with no exposure to the cans from light or elements, it will not break down for many years to come.

Glass Bottles: Same as cans, but way prettier. Glass bottles can become a work of art, melted down for more glass projects or recycled. I save the caps to reuse glass bottles for carrying my water around in. I do not like or choose to drink water out of plastic or buy it in plastic. This is a good idea to consider as store bought water has a lot of harmful additives in it. Glass is so beautiful. We have used it lately to create walls and planters as we do with the cans. You can also throw in bottles with your can projects that can act as windows into an inside space. You can combine glass bottles in patterns to create a stain glass affect in a room or in an outside structure such as a greenhouse or gazebo. Glass can also be cut in half and taped together into what we call 'brick bottles' to create light coming into a house from the outside and create healing colored patterns for your home. Again, reusing glass is beneficial for all. I also like the ideas I have seen to make used glass bottles into wine goblets and cups. You can reuse them by scoring the glass to take the top off. Or the bottom depending on which end you will use for your wine glass or cup. They have great YouTube videos on how to do this.

Glass Jars: If you buy mayonnaise, pickles, or anything in a jar, you can re-use them for storing food. I do my best when buying anything to think how I can re-use the jars, to store our pastas, beans, cereals, legumes, popcorn, spices, herbs, you name it! Great way to re-use glass jars. Also the smaller ones I re-use to put my Salve ointments into when I make them in the winter, or flip top bottles for my Tinctures to store them in. Vinegar bottles are great for storing homemade cleaners. And making funnels to percolate my tinctures with.

Reusing Building Materials: When endeavoring on any kind of project I typically look at recycled materials first for my building supplies. There is so much out there that is wasted, thrown away or ignored as a usable material. "One man's trash is another man's treasure." This is my truth. I love finding things to create with. When building our straw bale home years ago I found a man locally who saved used windows, doors, tiles, wood, sinks, and some plumbing materials to re-sell. And cheap! There is always that man in your community folks. People would change their minds after installing cabinetry or even appliances, tiles and more, either going to the dump or a re-store.

I wanted to save the big bucks to get the things I needed that I could not find used. I saved thousands by reusing items that were sitting around this guy's yard and would have eventually been brought to the dump if they were not spoken for and used somewhere else. Barn wood is another resource that is abundant. So many family farms are becoming abandoned and left to rot, sadly so. The resources on those farms are many. Metal sheeting, barn wood, all sorts of iron works lying around. There is enough to usually frame an entire house or line the walls with beautiful wood from one barn. Be mindful of up-scaling materials. Re-using helps so much to lessen the factory pollution and waste of buying new things. Recently I found an old iron door cover. A beautiful pattern but a part was broken off, so I use it now as a trellis for my rose plant. When I find things like that I really feel useful.

Reusing Bath Water & Using Rain Water to wash clothes:

I learned this easy way to wash clothes without having to use money or have a washer of my own. When I was on the road a lot as a young mother, we had to wash our clothes every few days. And having a young boy child it was a must. Using a five gallon bucket with reused bath water or rain water which we harvested by putting the bucket out by the edge of the roof or just outside when it heavily rained. Using Dr. Bronners soap, we washed our clothes in the bucket with a lid and plunger directly in the center of the lid. Cut out a hole that would fit the plunger snug. Then agitate the clothing by using the plunger up and down and in circles too. This helped a lot to save time and money by not needing to always go to the laundry mat. Simple washing and hang clothes to dry was and still is, a way to save on electricity, water and time! It actually takes less time to hand wash, than standing around waiting for an industrial machine to do the work.

There are a few other ways I washed clothes during this time of living simply. I once had a hand crank washer. It fit a good amount of clothes in it. It was small and did not need too much water to wash a load. You use your hand to crank it around a few times. Then it would rinse itself when you wanted by turning a small lever. Another way was an old fashioned hand cranking metal tub wash bin. It had a lot of room for a load of clothes. It had a hand lever to push back and forth to agitate, and a clothes ringer to ring the water out; all by hand. Then of course with any of these methods we hung our clothes on a line to dry.

I figured for centuries this is how we did our laundry so it can't be that bad. And it isn't. I actually enjoy doing my wash by hand rather than using my automatic washer. Even if we can limit the electric bill a little and use less water now and then, I think we could make a huge difference!

We also would reuse our bath water, and wash our clothes in our bath tub. This was before we had an in house washer. Of course if our bath water was super dirty we would not do this. The plants benefit from our bath water too in those situations. I would just add a few drops of Dr.Bronners and throw my clothes into the bath when I was done bathing, and use the bottom of the bath to beat the clothes up. Then ring out by hand and throw them on the line.

There are new inventions for washing clothes every day. I feel the simple ways are useful in case there are no other 'tools' available. Our next hand washer will be a foot pedals one. I am excited! Otherwise, we use our regular house electric washer and try to limit its use. In the winter this can be challenging sometimes, depending on the climate you live in. In our winter climate it is cold most days. But, luckily the sun can be out even on those days. So hanging up clothes is not as hard as it would be in other regions where it is mostly cloudy. If there is a way to hang up a line inside the house during the winter also helps. Maybe a wood stove is running to heat the home, or a fireplace. There are clothing racks also which help minimize the use of dryers. Therefore, minimizing your electric bill!

When building our home, we had a small one room cabin to live in with several other people. We used one metal bin to wash and one rack to dry. There was always a kettle of water on the wood stove. This made it easy to wash dishes or laundry in the bin at any time when needed. In the summer it was easier to wash in the bath tub outside. Try and see which ways work for you! You may feel that this is a great way to conserve water and electricity and find it actually may be a simple way to wash your clothes. And not only that, it feels more in balance with nature and feels good to know how to do these things.

Do it Yourself House Hold Items: Saving money is an essential part of creating a new paradigm in life. Eco-Friendly household cleaners, shampoos, remedies are a huge part of Eco-Awareness. To become a researcher, being confident and realizing that making your own cleaning and health care products are not only good for the environment and save you money, but they are wonderful for your health and the health of your children's future. Passing on knowledge and wisdom are the ancient ways of protecting ones family for generations to come.

It's basic thinking. It's about creating simplicity in your everyday life. We all clean, do laundry, brush our teeth, wash our bodies and hair. A few simple ingredients can help take care of almost all your basic everyday needs. Buy bulk ingredients, get reusable cloth. Get spray bottles or jars to store these in. Save old shampoo bottles to fill back up with your own shampoo and conditioners you can make yourself. Use small jars with lids for toothpaste, salves and lotions. Use dropper bottles for tinctures.

Some basic things to buy in bulk for making your homemade goods:

Baking Soda (A good kind like Bob's Mills without Aluminum)

Coconut Oil (A gallon of non-refined)

Jojoba Oil, Apricot or Almond Oil

Sesame Seed Oil (unfiltered)

Spearmint Oil (A high Quality brand that can be ingested)

Lavender Oil

Oregano Oil

Thieves Oil (Young Living)

Dr.Bronners Peppermint Soap

Himalayan Sea Salt

Apple Cider Vinegar

White Vinegar (Cheap kind is fine)

All these basic ingredients are a personal choice as to what grade or brand. If used on the body or in the mouth I would highly suggest getting high quality brands. Vinegar and Dr. Bronners soap can be good for laundry, dishes, cleaning the toilet, shower, bath, sinks, floors etc. I like mixing these two ingredients half and half then adding the rest of the spray bottle with hot water to clean. Adding Essential Oils for smell is always nice too! Thieves Oil (by Young Living Oils) is an excellent disinfectant for many things so I like adding that when cleaning and it smells pretty good also. Lemon Verbena, Lavender, and Oregano (Also a great anti-fungal-bacterial).

For hair, a simple way to wash is with Baking Soda and a drop of Essential Oil. Dr. Bronners is also a wonderful shampoo. None of these things are toxic and people rarely have sensitivity to them. A lot of people these days are chemical sensitive, as we are absorbing these chemicals into our bodies through our clothing, breathing them in and through our skin when cleaning. So many allergies and nervous system disorders can be related to the use of toxic chemicals in our home. Think simple. Use one basic cleaner for everything and you can't go wrong! If you feel it is time to get rid of any toxic chemical cleaners in your home, pause from reading this now. There is no time to waste! It is time to go clean out the crap. Get it out of your home and away from your family.

The Sacred Mouth:

Making your own toothpaste and mouth wash is a great way to get healthy teeth as well as avoiding additives in store bought pastes. An equal measure of coconut oil slowly melted down and baking soda with added drops of peppermint oil is great toothpaste. I usually put the coconut oil in a small jar in the window, so the sun can melt it. I do not overcook it, and then take it out as soon as it is melted to liquid and add the baking soda and the peppermint oil. It will turn solid again. I use a small wooden stick to scrape it out and put on my toothbrush.

A great tooth, gum and mouth cleanser is to use Sesame Seed Oil. After brushing with the coconut oil mix, I swoosh the Sesame Seed Oil in my mouth for a few minutes. This is called 'Oil Pulling.' You can literally feel the debris between the teeth and gums come out of your mouth when doing this. It feels so clean and I believe it helps whiten my teeth too! The Sesame Seed Oil is amazing to pull out toxins and debris from the mouth. Our mouths are a part of our immune system, this practice can benefit not only the local area of the mouth but our entire body's health.

These two ways of mouth care, for me, have improved my oral health and I believe are the reasons why I do not need to go to the dentist. My cavities have healed over time as well while doing this.

We use a very simplistic system to clean and care for our home. No allergies or skin disorders here. It is simple and less wasteful. Stop spending money on toxic chemicals which cause allergies, asthma, skin disease, cancer and so many more health issues.

You are your own health care provider

Making your own remedies for the common cold to serious health issues:

There are many ways to research and find what is good for your particular situation. I will not delve too deep into each one here as that is an entire book of its own. Finding salves, tincture and elixir recipes are easy now online. Books are great too, and there are amazing books out there with great recipes. It feels much more satisfying to make our own remedies than going to a Dr. to only find they have one prescription for everyone. Anti-Biotics, chemical made medicines, anti-depressants, and so called immunization shots. Which all contain byproducts of chemicals, animal and human cells and so much more deadly ingredients. Avoid whenever possible!

Homeopathy, herbs, energy, water, movement, creative expression and body work are all great ways to maintain health and heal most issues. Nutrition, care to rest and exercise are all vitally important for long term health. Mixed with all the other knowledge you have learned will make a huge difference in your well-being.

Water is also an excellent way to gain healing. Soaking in hot water with minerals added or essential oils can boost your mood, heal skin issues, help emotional upset and it is just a very relaxing way to heal the mind and body for many reasons. Our muscles and bones need to be rested and water is one of the best ways to do this. Because water is an anti-gravity space to float, our bodies can take time to heal without the added stress of gravity upon it. This is one of my favorite ways to heal and relax; especially when I am stressed or have pulled a muscle somewhere. Create time to relax in water whenever you can. If you live near a hot springs even better. We are fortunate to live near a few amazing natural hot springs.

Drinking water is also essential to health and long term vibrancy. Drinking clean and additive free water, not in plastic bottles, is an important factor in many health success stories. If our bodies have enough hydration, cell conductors, minerals and salts, the cells can rejuvenate and heal. Those who lack efficient hydration with the right compounds, tend to get sick more often and have a very acidic Ph. level in their bodies. To Alkaline the blood and hydrate well, make sure your water is tested for heavy metals and other pollutants before drinking an abundance of it. Getting a high quality filtration system for the home is one essential way to make sure you have clean water for your family.

Water is Life!

Chapter Five

Family Birth

Over the past few decades I have researched ways in which the family can provide care for one another in order to establish a Core Foundation. In the past, families relied on their own handed down recipes for dealing with ailments and natural functions such as birth, death and everything in between that came up.

After the medical establishment took over not that long ago in the scheme of things, they shoved out the folk healers, wise women and midwives with fear and threat tactics. Most submitted over time, to their ways of treatment. In birth this was a huge disaster. We hear of women and babies dying in the past from birth. And of course they still do. However, if we delve deeper into those stories of why that may have happened, it turns out that most of those stories were ones from that time, not long ago, of women entering into the hospital birth environment. The conditions and treatments of women and babies were more torture then any kind of scientific based care. It was an experimental phase, which is still taking place even today. The new found drugs and instruments may have caused these stories of birth being 'dangerous' and causing 'death'. Families prior to the birth industry survived many generations before medicalized birth. Today, in our country and in many industrialized countries around the world, most women give birth in hospitals. However, most babies are born at home in the majority of the world.

Because of military systems taking over to control population, and keep track of as many babies as they can coming into the world, western practices are taking over some of these areas where they had never known anything but birthing with their family. Separation of the family in birth is an unconscious act of violence. It controls and withholds the love and safety those mothers and babies have a right to experience at the time of birth. It is a way to subdued and detach people away from their own innate wisdom and family ties.

Mother and child in nature must attach and be very aware at the time of birth for survival and in order to thrive together. There is no species on our planet but humans who meddle in birth. All but us, have family births, attachment, immediate breastfeeding and bonding to only the mother herself. We have taken birth out of the family and institutionalized it to the point now where most women and their partners do not know or trust their own bodies or babies any longer. They place their bodies and babies into stranger's hands and hope for the best. And the best is whatever that system dictates. Our bodies then are not our own and become a part of the plan to detach our *'nature and nurture'* for mechanical material things, separating us from our source.

More and more women and their families are taking back birth; their literal *'birth right'* and human right to have care and love surrounding them for this special, sacred time. Birthing them with the same love and respect as they were created. Taking back the dignity and wisdom that reaches beyond into the next generations and for them to also have that knowledge to birth their own babies when that time comes.

Most do not realize that this evolution of family birth is more than just about the act of giving birth. It is practical, simple, real, raw and joyous. It also saves money, saves on the over use and abuse of drugs, procedures, staff and products related. The birth industry makes around 400 billion dollars per year. When we look back not even 100yrs ago, the cost of a birth was rather reasonable. Pay was possibly a trade or a few dollars, baked goods or a quilt. And many times nothing at all as women used to assist one another at this time, free of charge. They were Grandmothers, Mothers of the Mother, Sisters, dear friends who had babies themselves and sometimes Midwives later in history.

We also have to recall prior to the mid-20th century, most did not have access to our modern communications systems. No phones, no automobiles, no mass transportation. Therefore, most who birthed, most likely did so with family at home. Midwives may have made it to the births, may have missed them, or come after to help clean, cook and support the family. To get things done for the mother, so that she is able to rest and nurse her baby.

Today, the birth industry is something way over used. It costs tax payers and others as much as it would to house and feed the entire country. I am not saying that some women may not need a hospital. A few may need extra care and medical attention in pregnancy and birth, when they are ill or have serious health issues. When this is necessary it is useful to use the medical system. However, the amount of products manufactured to waste in the birth industry has taken a toll on the environment and on its consumers. The use of drugs, one use instruments, needles, plastic bags, tubes and other mechanisms are thrown away and it is piling up! They are polluting rivers, oceans and all the life that lives there. When having a baby, there is no need for most things. Only clean towels, clean water, maybe some herbs or extra hands in case needed. Most women can birth without much at all. And certainly without spending thousands of dollars doing so!

How the birth industry works today, is to place every mother and baby into a risk category and *'practice'* systematic procedures. Making others money in return. Our health, dignity, and our babies future depends on the time honored natural events of birth to even be here today. We all would not be here if it did not work well in the past.

To gather resources and support while creating a family is important. No one should have to suffer without support, education and resources today, in this highly resourceful environment. There are plenty of ways to help you find the proper care. The best care is from yourself first. It is only logical. However, finding the path in self-care is unique to each individual.

Before deciding to have a child, it is important to take excellent care of your mind, body and soul. Ask yourself if it is a good time to bring a child into your family. Talk with your partner, your family, your community, if that is where you feel you receive the best support. Are you able to take off work once the baby comes to spend time caring for him/her? Can you take care of yourself and avoid toxic relations? Growing a healthy baby, caring for you and a baby are the most important aspects of creating long term sustainability. If you find yourself in a situation that needs extra attention and care, there are ways to ask for help. Being mindful of the foundation you are creating to feel confident in all your choices of becoming a parent is a great start.

The Eco-Friendly Family begins with YOU. All parents want their children to be healthy and happy. How to create this is another story. It all begins with birth. Family is the core of that entire child's existence. If you have decided to raise awareness to the ways in which you can improve on your environment, grow and birth your babies into it, the rest is easy. Love is all you need. This comes with warmth, shelter, food, and support. Babies are born every minute of every day all over the world. Some people are more ready than others to be parents. The basics are right in your arms. Your dedication to your baby and family is the first step of creating this New World! Free of struggle, disease, poverty and injustice. *Ideally*.

Family birth and the Eco-Friendly Family go hand in hand. When we go deeper into the ways in which a mother births her babies, and how that affects each individual mother and baby and family; we will be able to understand why family birth is vitally important for the future of our planet and our own individual families. It is simple.

Our DNA depends on a few things. One is our heritage, where we derive from. Our ancestors and theirs are always a part of our inner cellular knowledge and wisdom. They made it and birthed more babies. And that is why you are here today, in this moment. If we interfere with the natural events surrounding birth, our cells are changed. Our DNA is shifted. After time, generations to come can be affected; maybe for the good, maybe not so good. When we drug and cut ourselves open to birth our babies, something shifts. The cells in our bodies and babies bodies change. They are affected in many ways. To be surrounded by a staff of strangers, told what to do or how to do it, given drugs to speed or slow things down, we are taking on the role of 'God'. We are basically saying we do not trust nature or our Creator and therefore let man take over the normal physiological functions we were meant to do on our own. This is a powerful message we send to our unborn babies. We cannot trust ourselves and we must lend ourselves over to the strangers. To take us and tell us how to do these things we were meant to do naturally.

Many families are taking their birth rights to this level of trust in themselves and their Creator to the place of birth. Families are making the choices to find out how they were made to care for and take care of one another in birth more and more. It is amazing when I am asked to help guide and support families on this journey. I am always so honored.

All we know is that birth must work because it is a part of everyday life and we are seven-billion on the planet to prove it!

Taking steps to plan for your ideal family birth:

First step is to be as healthy as you can. Eating clean foods, drinking clean water, and getting enough rest and exercise; take care to research your options of support.

There are many resources out there for the kinds of care you can give yourself or receive from others. Family birth does not mean all on your own, necessarily. It can mean that only your family is involved. It just depends on your needs. It could mean having a partner who studies and helps you find your needs and wants. Or it can be a female friend, mother, sister or even a midwife or doula. You do not have to choose anything you do not want. Some even see a medical Dr. during pregnancy and then give birth at home with their families or friends as support. If you find within your own heart, and ask your inner wisdom to give you some answers of how and with whom, or where or when, you will hear an answer. Your intuition as a mother is important on this journey into creation. The mother herself is the one who knows her own body and baby's needs, no one else can care for or make sure the mother is well but herself.

Even if you find you need a support system other than your family in birth, you may want to find ways to create the family birth with others involved. You are the boss. Always remember you are ultimately the one responsible and in charge of your body, birth and baby. No matter who else was hired or asked to be a part of your experience, you can create a joyous and simple drama free birth. Then if you find yourself in a situation where things did not seem to turn out the way you had wanted, you can flow with it and accept what comes next. You are the creator of this event. Be open to all possibilities.

An Eco-Friendly Family may be planning a drug free birth at a birth center. There is nothing wrong with choosing to birth in birth centers, even hospitals for that matter. If you truly need the medical attention. There is something to be said about having both the safety and comfort you feel you need during birth. However, we need to understand that these options are in fact not going to be easily experienced if you want a family centered event. Everyone's perceptions of situations are different. For one mother or family, the hospital or birth center was an amazing wonderful experience; for another, not so much. It depends on your needs, wants and desires for your birth. The baby also may need more time to remain attached to his/her umbilical cord. This can be a challenge in these environments. The blood to the baby is his/her lifeline. Stem cells are in the cord for a reason, to go into the baby at birth to protect him/her from future illness. When they tie and cut the cord in birth centers and hospitals, they are basically taking vital nutrients, stem cells and oxygen from that baby. A third of the baby's blood volume is lost and some have very difficult times breathing. Recovering red blood cells, creating immunity, and long term health issues result from this unnecessary procedure that is still standard practice in most hospitals and birth centers. Until those changes are made, a lot of Family Birthers will remain at home, sometimes alone to birth their babies, to protect them from these medical interferences.

There are so many interferences for insurance companies to take statistics of their hospital or birth center. Interfering with the natural events that should be able to unfold the way it needs to. By design we are made to survive birth so what is all the hoopla here? If you want a normal natural event to unfold in your birth, a family birth is optimal. Wherever you may choose to do this. If you can prepare, research, remain healthy in mind and body, this option may be a good one for you. Again, you are the boss of your body, baby and birth. Demand the change in any setting you may choose to have your baby's birth.

If you do not mind the shots of hepatitis B given to your newborn baby who is born with an immature liver to begin with, or the tests and procedures they do routinely at birth, eye anti-biotics etc. Or the interferences of strangers in and out of the room at birth. Maybe then it is not an issue for you. However, a lot of parents that I speak with would not want this kind of treatment done to them or their babies. I feel most people just have no idea what it is all about and that we are trained to think it is all 'ok' and just routine and necessary to have a 'good' birth or a 'safe' birth. Parents need to demand further evidence of anything, and everything before submitting to these so called safety procedures.

As parents we naturally want to protect our babies. The best way is to not let strangers interfere. Why would a stranger want to be a part of your personal birth experience to begin with? It is usually because it is their job. A job they chose possibly because they want to help others. But helping others can become a mundane and difficult practice. When we go in to see a practitioner of birth, we expect they want to help, care and are somehow interested in the betterment of our individual situation. But unfortunately this is rare. It is a business, nothing more in most cases. Our first investment is to ourselves. The way to paradigm shift in this world is to first take care of ourselves and our own. Our families depend on us to provide safety and protection against outside influences. In pregnancy and birth this is truer than anything else. We have invested time to create this little being and want the best care possible. Sometimes that care is best within our own hands and the hands of those closest to us.

When you find you want something raw, real and want to go deeper into your abilities as a family, it begins at this moment in time right now with you. If you can get pregnant and carry a baby to term, and take care of yourself, well, you most likely can birth just the same.

Breast Feeding for the Future

All Babies deserve the best start in life. We want them to be healthy and hopefully live long healthy lives.

The best way to ensure a great beginning of life is to breast feed our babies. It may sound simple, but in the last century there have been interferences from corporate investors of artificial nutrition for babies. It is a wonder why we have so many health issues today. The first food for babies should be the highest of quality. It should be the most sustainable for them. Mother's Milk is the one thing a mother can offer with no added plastics, chemicals and additives. She herself is the producer and makes milk specifically for her own baby's needs.

The first food in the breasts begins during pregnancy and proceeds to enhance as the child grows for their unique needs. The average time frame around the world for breastfeeding ones child prior to industrialized birth and feeding, was 3-7years. Those ages are no longer fed by the breast as much as they should be.

Newborns need the first milk which is called Colostrum. This is the highly dense protein packed clear liquid in the breast prior to birth and for the first few days after, before the milk slowly comes in. Colostrum is built of essential fatty acids for brain development; and bacteria for intestinal nourishment, for the newborn to survive while recuperating from the birth itself.

The action of breast feeding and the protective pro-biotics from the mother through her Colostrum, is essential for both mother and baby to be able to combat elements in the world. The newborns immune system is young. The birth itself, if natural and unhindered by drugs and machines can boost the chances for the baby to come into the world strong. Suckling is also extremely important as the newborn needs to release fluids in the lungs, ears, nasal cavities and swallowing is the second step to do this after birthing through the mother's body. Squeezing through the body of the mother is one step for the baby to activate their immune system and brain growth. Bacterium from the natural vaginal birth itself, is the first introduction to stimulate the baby's immune system, the second is suckling from the breast.

All mechanisms are vitally important for long term health. When the flow of milk begins around day three or four post-partum, the baby is ready internally to take on more food and less condensed proteins. The breast milk is made for that particular baby's needs. Whether that baby is premature or has a special needs issue, that milk is created by the mother for that child.

The intestinal tract is beginning to mature. So many vital organs and cellular developments are occurring rapidly. Even after only a few days, the newborn is beginning to develop their own antibodies and gut flora. It is important to have the correct nutrition to do this. The breast milk is not only essential for the internal growth and brain development but for cellular health. The cells in our bodies before and after birth are unique to our own biology. They can be disrupted if not fed appropriately.

Too many babies over the past century have been denied the most basic and essential part of their being here. Formula companies in cahoots with the medical birth industry have invested money and time to take mothers away from their birth rights to nourish their own. In turn, money is profited by many who do this. It is not our babies fault and not the mothers fault that this happened. However, we need to now step forth and make sure all babies get what they deserve, breast milk.

Even in rare situations when a mother cannot breast feed, there are others who will donate their milk or nurse that baby. The myth that was whispered to women back when they were beginning to birth in hospitals was that the babies were better off with 'clean' milk. Their own milk was not good enough. That the drugs during birth tainted them and their babies would benefit from the new synthetic, 'clean', man-made formulas they had developed for them. That it was 'savage' to breast feed. With the new modern technology, why bother. Too many mothers bought into this myth and gave up their bodies to science. And to the ones who dictated they were not good enough to feed their own babies, profited. This is a very sad situation.

Now because of this myth from long ago, so many mothers are told in one way or another that they are not fit to feed. It is still an issue today. All babies and mothers deserve the education and support to nourish them. Not only is this sustainable, it is vital for all of our survival on this planet. If we take into account the millions, if not billions of waste products out there; from manufacturing the formulas, the chemicals, additives and packaging and so on. It is a disgrace. And in the end, it is not good for our babies to be ingesting such synthetic and polluted substances. Or to live in an environment that replaces the Mother with machines.

Placental Preservation:

As in all things for our baby's future needs, being mindful and researching how easy it is to preserve your placenta, for the future health and well-being of your baby. Many families I work with and speak to around the world, use their placentas as a nutritive healing remedy after birth. They eat a small piece or much more, after it is born, while still attached to their babies.

Once the Placenta has done its job, whether that is after hours or days, they will also preserve it. The easiest way is to use a high quality sea salt to begin the drying process after birth. This may begin even if someone chooses a *'Lotus Birth,'* where the placenta and baby remain attached for hours or days until the cord dries and falls away on its own from the baby. There are many benefits in doing this. I will not delve too deep on this practice here. Rather, I want you to be able to understand how vitally important this is for your own health and your baby's health. The placenta is all of life, the *'Tree of Life'* as most of us in the birth world call it.

It is actually a very important and unique organ which the mother creates to sustain life. It is literally the only way we are even here today. Please research and find a way to honor and preserve the placenta for your future needs.

Chapter Six

The Challenges Ahead

The majority of society is not quite ready yet for this paradigm shift. I believe things are preparing it to be. At the same time, the challenges are rearing their ugly heads surrounding parents' rights, and the choices they make to become *Eco-Friendly Families*. Lately there has been much more government interferences with personal bodily rights being taken away. Bills trying to get passed to jail parents for refusing vaccines, and a case of a poor mother who was sent to jail because she protected her four year old son from being circumcised. Which later, the Father had him operated on anyway, court ordered. There are CPS calls on parents for having babies at home alone or not taking their kids to the Dr. for checkups. Many Challenges. All in all though, we have to remain steadfast. We are creating a shift in the ripples of this reality. It is going to combat us no matter what to some degree, until that reality ripples through others. Once the perception changes as a mass consciousness, which it will at some point soon, it will all be for a great cause. The future of our children and theirs.

Be strong. Don't give up! You are the one who can change this situation by living with your eyes open; to loving all creatures. Respecting and honoring all of the parts of you that are awakening to this Eco-Awareness. It is real and true. Nothing compares to the beauty here we were given to protect and nourish, not destroy and use up. The planet is not infinite with resources as we once thought. We continue polluting her rivers, oceans and skies. She is sensitive to us and our attitudes, and needs us to be more mindful than we have been. Much more.

Shifting our realities to where we can live simply and be a part of nature and all her wonders. Rather than fight her and work to only survive; wasting our precious time away from our first real work, our families. They are so important. So much so, if you have to live in a simple shelter with little comfort to be able to be with them, grow food with them, share time and love, it is worth every little bit of sacrifice. Working away from our babies or being apart from the ones who need us the most. To be cared for is *worth* the reward. The fullness of life is for us to be loved and share this world with the ones we love.

If you are someone who believes in manifestation, then let the manifestations begin. Thoughts are powerful. We can create our lives and even the surroundings by thinking positive. We cannot control everything. However, thought can create and manifest the world we live in. Literally. Everything, every kind of product or building or piece of clothing, is created by someone's imagination. If we are to re-create this world for the better, we can start by imagining it the way we would like if we could create it ourselves; beginning with *gratitude*. Honoring what is before us in this moment. Then we can begin to see how amazingly we can offer all our family and those in our lives such a wonderful vision. We can improve our personal and professional lives and our intimate and larger surroundings. All by using our greatest gift we were given, manifestation. The ways in which we can practice manifestation are vast. There are many areas in life which each one of us can choose to work on and learn how to do; and then passing on this skill that we all once had naturally to our children.

Before we were old enough to understand that dreams and magic were real, it was probably because no one told us they were not. When I was a small child, I remember my faerie friends and little creatures that I spent my day with. I would go sit under a large tree in my grandmother's back yard with a book and read to myself and my little friends would come and sit by me and communicate about their lives and it was real. I lost that magical realm once I realized those around me were not aware and I must be imagining it all. I went into a different realm of the difficult kind. Later when I was an adult and had my child, we re-connected. The magical realm of those who live among us returned to my vision and while raising my son, we both benefited. Because those so called creatures of a different realm are not seen by most, does not mean they do not exist. I felt it was important to acknowledge them and reunite with them in my adult life because they do serve a purpose. Creation and manifestation are real. We do it all the time. If we can slow down and listen to our spirit guides, faeries, trolls or gnomes more, then we can re-gain that childlike sense of being. And that is exactly what we need to create a New World, creative imagination!

peace on earth

Chapter Seven

Simple Solutions

Bring all your wisdom to the table. Don't hesitate and come with confidence. Now is the time to create solutions and live by YOUR TRUTH.

We are all here on this planet to share joy, create community, and raise our spirits to the next level. Learning and growing together so we can pass this on to the children so they too can have a home, garden and sustainability for many generations to come.

Our first mission is to learn how to live simply. Not wasting literal things or time on materials that do not sustain us. Find ten simple things you can eliminate and replace with something else or get rid of all together.

Write down ideas here:

Create a solution for two environmental issues you have in your personal life. An example for me would be cleaning with only hot water and soap or vinegar because anything else gives me skin disorders and makes me feel sick, giving me a headache. I want to have a clean home so I will use things that clean but also do not harm myself or the environment.

The other would be stress. I need to make sure I have a calm space to be able to feel supported and not stress out because that leads to high blood pressure for me. I will take time to have calm moments throughout the day. Walk outside in the garden or meditate, do yoga etc. This will help calm my nervous system so I am not frustrated or hypertensive. This benefits me to be the best I can be for my family and clients.

It could be anything that creates physical or emotional discomforts in your environment; figuring out how and what to give up. Making it better.

Practical things to consider for more Eco-Friendly Living

Composting food scraps:

Being a country girl at heart, and living in the mountains for well over two decades now, I have learned the best way to deal with food scraps is to compost them. There are a few reasons for doing this. First, it is a waste to throw food away in the trash at all. There is too much going into the landfills that cannot break down and go away naturally, but food will break down well in the ground. Another reason for us is that we honor our Mother Earth. We want to give back to her what she has given us, and in turn she feeds us her fruits. Literally our food compost will help our food grow, trees, bushes and vegetable gardens all benefit from our food waste.

This for us is also ceremonial. When we give the earth back the food we took from her, it is an offering and it does count. Other reasons include creating soil and helping little critters out with food; possibly creating alkaline or more acidic soils in some areas. Depending on your conditions, you could have rich nutritious soul made from your food scraps within a few weeks' time and in turn be able to grow wonderful food at home from it.

Compost is simple. Find a sunny spot. 3x3 space is sufficient. Dig a few feet down in a circle or square. Put chicken wire around that space creating a tunnel about four feet off the ground. Begin with your food scraps, putting them in the hole. Make sure there are no meat products in there. You may need to give those to a dog or put in another system. Some fermentation can occur when burying meat on its own and then using it later in the compost pile.

After you have a layer of your food scraps in your compost hole, either use leaves, grass clippings (good for nitrates) or straw to layer them. Woodchips or any kind of organic matter around your yard will work as well. We sometimes use our ashes from the fireplace too. Make sure to keep the compost moist and cover it with a black trash bag or tarp. This way, it will break down quicker with heat from the sun, moisture and darkness. If you have chickens, feed them some of the scraps too.

Reusing water: Another great way to conserve on resources and save a bit of money is to reuse water. The way I find this works, is to do as much as possible. Instead of dumping water down our drains all the time when we are done with a bath or have some extra water left over from cooking or in our glasses, we water our plants with it. We have a bucket in the back room we store water in, that is extra water from the baths or sink and use it to flush the toilet. Some have shared that they do not have water coming into their toilets. They only use used water, to flush by pouring water in it when they need to flush after pooping. We do not flush when we pee, only poop. This also saves a lot of water. No reason to flush our own bodily water, urine is fluid. Why use a gallon of water to flush water?

Make your own toilet paper: I have done this in my youth before we had recycled toilet paper out there. We found clothes at thrift stores or used our own clothes we did not want anymore and cut pieces of cotton and flannel to make butt wipes. We rinsed them into a small bucket with soap and vinegar before washing. The poop was separated into the toilet. Basically shook off into it, like a cloth diaper system. We reused these pieces of fabric over and over until they were no longer usable and then they went into a hole with other compost materials. Baby wipes can be made the same way. They are softer and do not have chemicals like store bought baby wipes. And they are free to make. Simply cut pieces of fabric. Then have a small spray bottle of warm water and your favorite essential oil with a few drops of Dr. Baby Bronners soap. This can be used to spray your baby's butt and wipe it with the cloth. Throw into a separate bag to take home and wash. Not hard, saves money and is healthier for the baby and environment. Too many conventional baby wipes are thrown in the trash or down toilets.

Shop Local: There are still local farmers markets for produce and local made dairy products.

Before you head out to shop, to buy stuff you may or may not need, think about shopping local. Local privately owned stores or thrift stores are truly the Eco-Friendly ways to put back a small bit of money into the community and save on pollution from factory made new items. You can also save money by purchasing used materials, clothes, kitchenware, furniture and so much more! Craft supplies and fabric are always on the shelves at the thrift shops that I shop at.

It is wise and also conservative to think before buying from corporate chains like Walmart or Target. They create so much pollution, slave labor, and generate money to produce more of the same. From my standpoint, what does it really matter if I buy used? I can feel good about reusing something someone has donated and paying back into an organization or foundation that gives back that money to a good cause'. Most thrift shops help the less fortunate with employment and education. Using second hand products helps in many ways. It reduces production pollution and waste. It also feels good to be able to save money on things that would normally be twice or more times expensive. Family owned and operated shops are also a great place to shop.

When working on finding a local farmer for food or growing your own, think about trading. I traded my crafts and food from my gardens for other items I did not produce. Yes, people still do this. Ask around.

Separating Trash: Most of us today know about recycling. However, taking our plastics, cans and glass to the recycling center is not always productive. Some of those things end up not being recycled at all. Some go to the regular dump and some get taken away to be manufactured again and again. This is also not that efficient in the long run. Minimize your trash and try to buy things you can reuse. Look at packaging before buying things. Can you reuse the packaging or somehow compost it, burn it, or make a project out of it? We do our best in our home by separating things into categories. I like to use glass bottles and aluminum cans for outside projects, planters, walls, etc. Plastic bottles can also be used. I save the strong ones for that. All paper is saved for cleaning, fire starter and compost. Plastic containers are reused for food storage and seed starts. The plastic wrappers, when we have those, are put into a plastic bag which we take to recycle. Or they can be used to weave more bags.

We try to minimize our trash to one small bag per week, but are constantly working on less waste. Figuring out that each time we buy something there is waste made. We reuse plastic bags for the trash instead of buying trash bags all the time, sometimes we do buy them but we limit them.

Shopping bags: Make your own shopping bags. Use old clothes, fabric or even thread to make your own shopping bags. Or buy some reusable ones. I have made ones out of used yarns from thrift shops, left over fabric from clothes or sheets I have saved for various uses. It does save quite a bit of waste from the manufacturing of plastic or paper bags in the markets. I have seen creative recycled plastic bottle bags and canvas ones too. A lot of people do not realize that doing a simple thing like reusing shopping bags, helps the planet by reducing pollution and waste at the landfill. If everyone did this one simple thing, we would see a huge reduction of trash at the dump. It would take several decades of doing this but eventually we would see the change. I would encourage everyone to visit their local landfill at least once to see what we are doing by throwing away so many things and not reusing or recycling. It is a very sad sight!

Energy: Most of us have running water, electricity, plumbing for waste, etc. In our homes, we can lessen the use of all these things by being aware of the bills that come in. We can do our best to limit use by turning off lights when not needed, getting low energy efficient bulbs, and turning off the television when we are not watching it. We do our best to conserve any amount of energy used. Washing clothes and drying them on a line outside on sunny days. I know for a fact, this alone helps minimize my electric bill a lot. Washing with cold water instead of warm or hot all the time. Things still get washed just fine. Hand washing dishes and towel drying them. I have not used a dishwasher in many years and I feel they get done just as well as any machine.

Changing some habits to conserve on our energy use is sometimes easier than it seems. We need to just rewire our brains to do things a little differently; instead of letting bath water go down the drain, save it for flushing the toilet or watering plants. We can all do these simple things to lessen consumption. You can go even further and go off grid. Put a composting toilet in your home. Go solar or wind. Reuse water for outside areas by installing grey water lines. Create rain water catchments to use for gardens or watering animals. All these things can be done and will have an impact on *our* Eco-System.

Food: The best way to save money and benefit your health is to grow your own food. You can grow a small plot of food in your yard or in a box on a porch or even in a sunny room in your home. Doing this can reduce the risk of so many issues. One is our health. Home grown food is yours, your seed to plate and no handling or chemicals or extra charges and plastic wrap to deal with. Most store bought food is shipped from a place where we do not live. It is handled by many hands, and sprayed with stabilizers and additives which are not good for our bodies. Food sits on shelves for many days, or even weeks before being consumed. This is not natural or normal for our bodies to take in. It is not live food. Even if you can only grow a few greens, this would help the body maintain good cell production and live enzymes for immune function.

Try to find a local farmer, someone who does not use chemicals to grow food. This is true for dairy and meat as well. No hormones or *anti*-biotics needed. If you can buy local and grow some simple greens you will again, save money and eat for your health. It is quality not quantity that counts with food. The more live food you eat the less hungry you will feel. The food that sits around is not alive and can only fill you to a certain point and you then are hungry again because your body needs live food to sustain and maintain cell production. I find if I eat live fresh food, the less hungry I get.

Driving: If you are like most people on the planet who own a car, you probably drive almost every day; either to work or to the store. There are ways to lessen the use of cars and fuel and all that entails driving. Try to find partners to ride with to work. Take a form of public transportation, walk, ride a bike, train, bus, and commute less. The pollution that we create driving can not only cause smog and poor air quality, but stress on the planet, stress on ourselves and it is not a very safe way to travel. We have figured out how to limit our driving when only necessary. Asking for assistance at times when others we know like neighbors, family, or friends are going to the store or to the city to get supplies. We save on gas and share the trip when we can so there is less need to use the car to go anywhere. Luckily we have jobs that do not take us away from home every day. If you or your partner has to go out every day, maybe there is an alternative to driving or maybe they can share a ride with someone. Lessen our fuel consumption for the air quality and our children's future health.

Getting others on board!

One tool some families use is to make this a fun transition to do together. It would be fun to make a game out of it. Create a list of things you would like to see change, like lowering energy bills and use of utilities. Set a precedence to show all the utility bills to the family and ask which ones each would like to help lower or eliminate. This could mean someone giving up a particular past time, like playing video games. Using too many lights when not needed, or turning off a cell phone or computer each day for an allotted time. Maybe consider sharing a family phone or computer for a while. The goal would be to learn how to lessen energy consumption and bills. Also to have facetime, actually face to face!

The money saved each month from the changes made could turn into a reward. Those savings could go into a family trip or buy a treat or maybe even to buy seeds to plant and grow some family food.

It can be a fun game for the family to play together and in return, the rewards would be for the children to be able to go through life with an awareness of how we impact our world by our consumption choices. Over time, this practice will become normal and standard. This is a great way to teach responsibilities for our children; to grow up aware of the reality of energy use and how to limit it; by learning to make good choices for themselves and their families in the future.

Not everyone has to be totally on board with the way we think or feel about the environment. But we all have awareness that something needs to be done. And the time is now. There is no time to waste. When, for the past few generations, all we have been doing is wasting time and energy and polluting our planet. The last few generations did not know or did not want to know, how their choices were affecting generations to come. Now we do know that our future depends on how we behave and how we care for this planet. Our children's children deserve a clean place to live. Breathe air that is not toxic or eat food without pesticides and genetically modified poisons. They deserve to grow and eat fresh foods and live simply, within nature and co-exist ecologically with all living beings. I know it can be done. I think with some tools and some understanding of how we affect one another, the planet and its future for these next generations coming, we can make a difference.

At this time, things are changing rapidly. Technology has taken over most of our lives with iPods, pads, iPhones, computers, etc. Everything is remote. We are like walking remote controllers. We do not look at people any longer. Discussions are through texting or emailing. We do not write letters anymore with cute stickers and stamps. It is getting way out of control. As sad as this is, it is what it is, and to be able to remove oneself from the madness is not easy. Let us sit and think about how we can limit or eliminate this issue. Put the phone down or the computer, iPod or Pad. Try to go outside without any cell phone or device once a day for a week. Go play in the dirt, garden, play with the kids and leave the phone somewhere where you cannot hear it or see it. Doing this for several hours a day every day for a week if you can. Note any emotional, mental or even physical sensations of letting these things go. If you are addicted to the devices, increase your time away from them by one hour each day. As crazy as it may sound, we did not always have these devices. Our brains were not naturally wired to take in so much radiation and electronic frequencies each day, every day. We were not programmed to only communicate through text or internet. We used to actually sit and talk face to face, use phones to call people or write a handwritten letter, which took much thought and focus. Our brains were working on a different level than they are now.

Some of today's technologies are more or less useful, making our lives easier. However, they are becoming harmful and making us 'zombies' and disconnected from others and ourselves. The smallest children are using these devices as though they are harmless; when all the exposure to the electronic frequencies is, in fact, changing their brain structures. And they are also becoming addicted. They are too young to combat such addiction. They beg and plead to play one more game, on the iPad or phone. They freak out, and we do not understand because we did not have this issue when we were their age. We played outside, rode our bikes, went over to friends and had camp outs in the back yard under the stars. It is rare to see this now. Playing outside has turned into playing video games inside for hours at a time. TV is an issue too. I for one was a TV junkie as a kid; single mom at work syndrome. I understand the dilemma. It is not easy being a parent. We need time to ourselves too. But now it has become the past time for so long and too many. Let's begin to shift the technological family to the Eco-Friendly Family.

Chapter Eight

Saving Our Planet for Our Kids

Personally, I would like to see the future as a vast and green sustainable loving place for my grandson. He means the world to me. My grandson is young. He is four and has no idea yet what this planet will look like for his children to come. I hope and pray each and every day that things here in this beautiful place will improve. That politics will be more logical. It should be *"for the people, by the people."* I visualize a world where parents make babies in love and raise them with the awareness to thrive and preserve resources. That everyone will have healthy food to eat and homes to stay warm in. A world where water and all natural resources are not abused and over used. That the wealthy would begin helping the poor to build homes and teach self-reliance and sustainability. I want to see an *Eco-Friendly* World for the future of my grandson and those to come.

"Let us walk softly on the Earth with all living beings great and small remembering as we go, that one God kind and wise, created all." ~Indian Blessing

Remembering, that is a quote I received from the Lakota Sioux yesterday in the mail. As I was writing this book I received this. I find things to be in alignment some days and this was something that I was trying to articulate in this book already. This hit it straight on!

We all want deeply to protect our children. We want them to be happy. We want them to be healthy. It is not unusual for a parent to want these things. So we buy them stuff. We take them to the Dr. for every little thing. We push food on them day and night. We give them what they want so they don't cry. It is not unusual to want them to be happy and to not let them leave your sight. There comes a time though when we need to ask ourselves what is best for their future health, future planet and future emotional well-being. Physically we want to protect them from harm at all times. What about teaching them to care for themselves by caring for the planet and all its creatures that inhabit it?

In my opinion, we are not doing our children justice by giving in to the consumer mentality. Most kids are very healthy when they are held, sung to, massaged, played with outdoors, fed well, and loved! They only need the basic necessities. They do not need a million plastic toys they will probably never play with. That are toxic and hazardous to their health. They probably don't need candy, soda and ice cream to be able to fall asleep at night. Likely, kids will not even know about computer games, iPads and phones unless those around them use them. It is what we as parents choose to expose them to that will set the stage for their entire lives. If we are going to shift the paradigm of this world and start creating a cleaner, more loving sustainable environment for our kids, we need to begin with ourselves. We are the ones setting the example and planting the figurative and literal seeds of the future.

Each generation has its flaws of incorporating something new that later becomes known to be bad or good or really bad or good. Our last few generations have a huge flaw that is now known to cause harm. This one I feel is how we birth our children. 98% of the United States babies are born in the hospital. All these babies are potentially being harmed by unnecessary and unneeded procedures, drugs and operations. They are given vaccines before leaving the hospital and three other drugs on average before they are even twenty four hours old. This alone can cause long term harm.

To save the future of our planet for our children and theirs, we must first learn how to preserve the most precious stages of life. Conception, pregnancy and birth are the first. Becoming pregnant and being as healthy as you can before and during will be a great start. You can research many options and support systems for having the most interference free pregnancy and birth possible. This will lessen the chance of the baby receiving all these early dangerous procedures and treatments and hopefully avoiding long term health issues and mental and emotional ones too. Do your research on procedures in pregnancy and birth. Find a great holistic support system and keep things as natural as possible. Eat healthy food and drink clean water.

Final Thoughts:

Today's Eco-Friendly Family faces many challenges. I do not feel it will be impossible to re-create our paradigm or structure. It will take ALL of US; as many as possible at least, to do so. As a group we can shift things. We have in the past and we can now.

Just remember, YOU and YOUR FAMILY are important! It is vital for us to preserve this planet, our Mother Earth, for our children and theirs. We cannot walk around blind to the pollution, waste, food and water tampering any longer. We need to stand up and take action by not participating in the destruction of our great planet!

Just say *No!* to anything that does not serve the greater good of all. In turn, living simply and saving money is a great way to be, and to be able to do other things or help others to have the basic needs they also deserve. We are one great Eco-Family on Earth.

We share this amazing planet and can love her and all who inhabit her while we are still here. The Oceans, Rivers, Lakes, all the Forests and Animals that live in them and here with us, need us!! Our children and their children need us to take this seriously and do the best we can. Teach them to learn how to take care of our mother before she is not able to care for us.

YOU ARE VERY IMPORTANT TO THE FUTURE OF OUR PLANET AND YOUR CHILDREN'S CHILDREN!

We are in this Together!

Recipes:

Shampoo:

Coconut milk ¼ cup
Dr. Bronners Castile Soap 1/3 cup
Essential Oils 20 drops of what you like. Rosemary, Lavender, Peppermint, Lemon, Orange, and Lime whatever you desire!

Conditioner:

Coconut oil 1 cup
Jojoba Oil 1 tsp
Olive or Vitamin E Oil 1 tsp
5 Drops of Lavender oil or any oil that you desire!

Cleaning: This is for multi-use

2cups of warm water in spray bottle
2cups of white vinegar or apple cider vinegar
2TBS of baking soda Or Peppermint Dr. Bronners Soap.
Essential Oils of Orange, Lavender, Lemon Verbena or Balm, Thieves, Peppermint or whatever you desire!

Use for counters, toilet, shower, tubs, sinks, Laundry, Dishes, some floors, as an air freshener.

Skin Moisturizers:

1cup Coconut Oil, 1tsp Vitamin E, ¼cup Jojoba 1/4cup Oil, 1/4cup Sesame seed Oil, 1/3 cup Apricot Oil, 20 drops Lavender Oil.

Mix in on a warm low heat or in a jar. Put all ingredients in a sunny window for a few hours. Stir and let stand or put in the refrigerator until solid.

Essential Herbs for The Home: These plants are easily grown in most climates and can come back each year as they multiply and create beauty. They are beneficial in many ways on their own or combined with other herbs. Use in salves, tinctures, and body products that you can make on your own. These are basic herbs which can uplift moods and calm the spirit when needed! They can be grown in the ground in most soils and are basic essentials for health and healing. LOVE YOUR PLANTS.

Comfrey: So many uses for cuts, healing bones, and healing internal issues.

Rosemary: Great for cooking, making antiseptic compresses, vinegars, lotions, and hair treatments. Smells good too!

Yarrow: Immediate use for cuts and fevers. It is great for salves and teas. Used with other herbs can help various skin conditions and is a great antiseptic.

Catnip: Dried for teas is very calming for the nervous system and mental exhaustion. Use the fresh plant for food like pesto's and in salads. It can boost your energy. Cats love it.

Lemon Balm: Aromatic lemon smell. It is very calming and tasty. In teas dry it can relax and calm a person down from a hard day. Just the smell alone can lift ones mood!

Peppermint: This is wonderful in homemade products for cleaning to hair treatments. It can be dried for teas or fresh infusions. It is a wonderful smelling mood lifting plant.

Chamomile: A wonderful aromatic, calming, edible flower that is easily grown in most climates. As a dried herb it is made into teas and can be a wonderful addition to any salad when fresh.

Think simply about life. **In-Joy** it, and share it with your families!
The best life is one full of love and laughter. Nothing in this world is
more important than caring for our Mother Earth and our loved
ones.
They are one in the same.
You are worth the effort and to be honored!

Many Blessings & Much Love,

Zuki

www.ingramcontent.com/pod-product-compliance
Lightning Source LLC
Chambersburg PA
CBHW031524040426
42445CB00009B/386